——The Coast of——
MAINE

The Coast of — MAINE

Photography by
Wayne Barrett
and
Anne MacKay

Introduction by
Christina Tree

SKYLINE
PRESS

ACKNOWLEDGMENTS
Our special thanks are due to Jack and Louise Fernandez,
Lester Braddock, the Bohndell Sails and Rigging Company,
the Stanley Brothers of Monhegan Island, and W.H. McElvain.
WAYNE BARRETT and ANNE MacKAY

Produced by Roger Boulton Publishing Services, Toronto
Designed by Fortunato Aglialoro

©1984 Chicago Review Press, Incorporated
SKYLINE PRESS is an imprint of Chicago Review Press

ISBN 1-55652-087-5, previously 0-19-540610-9
Printed in Hong Kong by Everbest Printing Company, LTD,
through Four Colour Imports, LTD.

Introduction

Maine may have the crookedest coastline in all the world. As the gull flies, the distance from Kittery to Eastport is just 225 miles. But as it tacks and jibs its way in and out of coves, inlets, reaches and bays, the shore measures more than 3500 miles.

Here men have always boated—rather than walked—from neck to point—with reason: it's usually the shortest way to get from place to place. From Eastport to Lubec, for instance, it's three miles by boat, 40 miles by land. From Rockland to Stonington it's 100 miles by road, but just 22 miles across Penobscot Bay.

And getting there, barring fog or other weather, is usually more pleasant by sea than by land. Sailors, in fact, come from afar each summer just for the pleasure of gliding through Penobscot Bay—the crookedest and deepest of all the indentations along the Maine Coast. Obviously designed with yachtsmen in mind, it is studded with islands and offers dozens of snug harbors, some of them wonderfully hidden.

Geologists have an explanation for this delightful blending of land and sea. They tell us that in the big melt following the ice ages, as the land slowly stabilized, the range of coastal hills that trails south from Canada almost to Portland remained partially drowned. Today only the ridgelines hump above the water—in the shape of those peninsulas which stretch south from Route 1, like so many fingers pointing out to sea and to the 2000 or so islands (once knolls and hills) which are scattered off-shore.

This is the 'rockbound coast' conjured up by the mention of Maine. Nowhere else on the eastern seaboard do mountains meet sea in the way they do on Mount Desert or at Camden. Nowhere else do tides vary as widely (30 feet in Passamaquoddy Bay) or narrow peninsulas take you as far out to sea (Stonington, linked to the coast road by bridges, is still a full 40 miles south of coastal Route 1).

What you don't see, of course, are the sunken valleys just off-shore, the drowned landscape which has long made an ideal breeding ground for lobster, shrimp, scallops, cod, mackerel, haddock, tuna, bass, salmon and other fish.

The people attracted by this lie of land and sea have always been sailors and fishermen rather than farmers. They have always spoken of home as 'Downeast', a nautical term meaning sailing with the prevailing winds, which dependably blow from the southwest, thus ushering sailing vessels ever eastward.

The precise location of the true 'Downeast' is another question. For most out-of-staters it tends to mean wherever they summer in Maine, probably Ogunquit, the Kennebunks or one of the other Southern Coast beach resorts. And the Bar Harbor Chamber of Commerce (211 miles up Route 1) touts Mount Desert as 'Downeast' writ large—the end of the rainbow as well as the tourist trail. But those superior summer people with homes in Hancock County just north of Bar Harbor know where it's at.

'You don't know what it means to be Downeast until you have crossed the Sullivan bridge', a convert to Gouldsboro tells me. The Sullivan Bridge, be it said, is a rusty span which Route 1 traverses *en route* to the Schoodic Peninsula, the easternmost finger of land on which out-of-staters have roosted in sociable numbers. Its 'Point' is the less visited part of Acadia National Park.

Beyond Milbridge, however, no one argues. You are definitely 'Downeast'. Trawlers and lobsterboats (not sailing vessels of any size) are what you see in the harbors, and work is so seasonal (raking blueberries in August, making wreaths in November, digging for clams and seaworms, lobstering, fishing, whenever you can)—and scarce—that if you don't bring the work down with you, you'd better not think of settling in.

The truth is that the more you search for your own 'Downeast'— that perfect inlet with high-roofed homes, yards brimming with lupins, the country store with gas pumps out front and lobster traps in the back—the more you are amazed by how often this grouping is still repeated, by how much 'unspoiled' beauty survives along the entire coast of Maine.

From the moment you cross the Piscataqua you know you are in Maine. Right there in Kittery you find walls of pine trees. Right there on Gerrish Island you find lobster traps piled up next to weathered fishing shacks, not that different from the lobster traps piled up next to fishing shacks at Cutler Harbor, some 20 miles from the Canadian border. Along Route 1 the motels, outlets and assorted tourist traps are thicker in some places than in others but they are to be found all the way from Kittery to Eastport, telling you every quarter-mile that you are 'Downeast' in *Maine*, MAINE, MAINE. And the real article is never far from Route 1, especially east of Casco Bay where the peninsulas begin, each its own narrow land of twisty roads, pointed firs and unexpected inlets. The fact is that this entire ragged, rugged coast is a land apart, shaped not only by glaciers but by its own very peculiar history.

Schoolchildren in the rest of America may learn that the pilgrims were New England's first settlers. In Maine they know that long before the pilgrims built their stockade at Plymouth both a settlement and a boat had been built at the mouth of the Kennebec River. English merchants had set up fortified fishing stations at Pemaquid Beach; also at Winter Harbor, Castine, Damariscotta, Biddeford Pool and on Monhegan. French missionaries had already established a foothold on Mount Desert; its destruction had triggered the tensions that quickly divided the land into English territory south of the Penobscot River and French territory to the north of it.

In Maine you learn that it was only with the help of the Indian Samoset's corn which he had stored at his Pemaquid home, also with supplies from English merchants already established at Pemaquid, that the Pilgrims survived the winter of 1622. And it was with the proceeds of beaver pelts traded at Cushenoc (an Indian village on the present site of Augusta) that they managed to pay off their debt to their English creditors.

By 1640 there were already some 1400 white men living between the Piscataqua and Penobscot rivers and an unrecorded number farther east—not a particularly religious lot but including some larger-than-life men whose legends you still meet; men like the Baron de St Castin, a young French nobleman who married a Penobscot princess and set up his own fur-trading station at Pentagoet (now named Castine). When this was destroyed by an English frigate in 1688 it's said that the Baron himself took to the warpath, leading Indian attacks on dozens of villages, setting back Maine's settlement by at least three decades.

Castine itself is a fine example of this coast's stormy, little-known history. According to the historical markers, posted everywhere around this serene yachting haven, the town has been claimed by four different countries—including the Dutch. During the Revolution its Tory residents (most of them fled to this outpost from Portland and Boston) welcomed the British who set to building a Fort George. When the infuriated Commonwealth of Massachusetts retaliated by sending a huge fleet (eighteen armed vessels and twenty-four transports) the British actually managed to defeat them. Far from trying to forget this embarrassing incident, the State of Maine has made the old British barracks the site of its Maritime Academy.

In Machias, of course, you learn that the first naval battle of the Revolution was waged off-shore on 12 June 1775 by the small sloop *Unity* against the British man-of-war *Margetta* and that this time the local patriots won.

In the War of 1812 the British again took possession not only of Castine but of all Maine to the East. Only in 1814 was the border with Canada agreed. Plainly Maine is nearer to Canada than it is to Washington and many stories tell how the seafaring lives of Canada and Maine are intertwined. In the museum on Little Cranberry Island you learn of a local captain who finished hauling for cod off Newfoundland, then lost his way in the Newfoundland fog—luckily coming to safe harbor in Oporto, Portugal, 3500 miles away, where he sold his cod and loaded up with enough salt to buy himself a schooner when he got home.

In 1820 the Massachusetts District of Maine became a state of the Union, planting its white pine in the middle of its new seal. This launched an era during which the ocean of forest in their back yard supplied coastal craftsmen with the wood to build ships to sail the ocean in their front yard—an industry which increased with the scarcity of lumber farther south.

Logs were floated down from the north woods on the Kennebec and Penobscot rivers. From the boom town of Bangor they were shipped off in the shape of lumber to far ports. In dozens of coastal towns they were shaped into ships. A total of 5000 ships have been launched from Bath shipyards alone over the years.

Maine men of course sailed those ships—some of them, as was the habit in the town of Searsport, bringing their entire families along and taking home ideas as well as souvenirs.

'A ship-building, a ship-sailing community has an unconscious poetry underlying its existence', wrote Harriet Beecher Stowe in *The Pearl of Orr's Island*. 'Exotic ideas from foreign lands relieve the trite monotony of life; the shipowner lives in communion with the whole world. . . .'

The impressive captains' homes in villages like Thomaston, Wiscasset and Kennebunkport suggest imported sophistication and treasures within—the kind of intricately carved Chinese chests now displayed in the Penobscot Maine Museum at Searsport and the South Seas trophies to be seen in the Maine Maritime Museum at Bath.

Bath itself has made the transition to steel-hulled vessels. The Bath Iron Works' 400-foot-high shipways crane looms over the city and this shipbuilding company remains the largest single employer in Maine.

But shipbuilding is way down the line of today's coastal industries. By the mid-nineteenth century steamers and trains were already ushering in a new era for the Maine coast, bringing summer visitors.

As early as the 1830s a summer hotel had been built at Old Orchard Beach, where the water had long attracted local farmers who believed in its curative powers. Then in 1836 a bridge was built, connecting Mount Desert with the mainland. Immediately artists began crossing the bridge and were soon followed by 'summer rusticators'. Then came the steamboats, putting previously isolated islands and peninsula tips at the end of a luxurious overnight cruise from Boston—with rail connections to New York and the rest of the country. And in 1854 the Grand Trunk railroad brought Montreal within a day's ride of Old Orchard Beach.

More than 200 millionaires built grandiose summer homes on Mount Desert and others grouped themselves in similar shingled cottages on Campobello Island, at Prout's Neck and York Harbor. More modest compounds mushroomed up and down the coast and on the islands; often they were built by people who had been neighbors somewhere else—like the cluster of gingerbread cottages on Eggemoggin Reach that were all owned by friends from Cincinnati. Huge summer hotels were built by the splendid beaches in the Yorks, Kennebunks and Ogunquit, even on islands like Peaks, Chebeague and Monhegan. City mill-workers flocked to Camp Meetings like that sponsored by the Free Baptists in 1881 at Ocean Park.

This is the Maine that Winslow Homer painted—the bathers and the sea that was now a fashionable infatuation. The period can still be sensed best on Monhegan, a magnificent island with steep cliffs and tall pines. Here Thomas Edison's grandson led a fight against a major summer development which would entail installing electricity. The island still has no electricity and private phones came just this past year. Yet summer people find their way here by the ferry-load—the day-trippers out on the balmy days from Boothbay Harbor and the earnest artists, birders and botanists who come on the *Laura-B* from Port Clyde to spend weeks wandering the woods and headlands.

Maine's first tourist tide ebbed with World War I. It returned after the war but in a way that changed the character of coastal places. Those were the days when every American had to buy a new car and, it seemed, to drive it up Route 1—which began sprouting 'trading posts', 'lobster pounds', and 'motor courts'. More elaborate motels and motor inns proliferated during a similar car boom after World War II. In recent years there has been a new demand for the old surviving summer hotels, smaller inns and newly burgeoning 'Bed and Breakfasts'.

Three-fourths of the people who vacation in Maine stick to the Coast and more than half of these go only as far as the beaches which scallop the shore south of Portland. The 'tourist crunch' then, such as it is, is confined to the 35 miles between Kittery and Portland, more precisely to the Yorks, Ogunquit, Wells, Kennebunkport and Old Orchard Beach.

Yet, thanks to the temperature of the water, few Maine beaches are really crowded. Even at Ogunquit there is always space on the firm sand to fly a kite and for children to learn to swim, the way I did, in the warmer Ogunquit River.

Countless families have summer-in-Maine rituals which pass from generation to generation. Each summer I find myself sitting on the same rocks by Ogunquit Beach that a photo shows my grandmother posed against *circa* 1930. I watch my children breathlessly select lobsters from the same concrete holding tank I scanned as a child, consume them at the same swinging tables, pestered by the same flies. I remember my own first wonder at a tidal pool—the starfish, sea lettuce and limpets trapped in the shallow pools below the Marginal Way. Once again I find myself content to sit all day on the rocks—or in a canoe in Scarborough Marsh, scouting for a Great Blue Heron, Snowy Egret or Glossy Ibis.

Even in Kennebunkport's busy Dock Square or amid the match-box beach cottages of Wells Beach you are just a walk away from uncluttered, unpeopled places where sand and sea meet.

North from Portland there are only three real resort towns—Boothbay Harbor, Camden and Bar Harbor—spaced like a giant's stepping stones. The lure in Boothbay Harbor is, of course, its choice of boat excursions and its hidden, warm-water ponds. Camden is departure point for half of the Windjammers, those grand schooners—some brand new, one (the *Stephen Taber*) dating back to 1871—which introduce landlubbers to the glory of sailing Penobscot Bay. Bar Harbor, of course, is just a staging ground for Acadia National Park, which encompasses most of Mount Desert, for its seventeen mountains which rise abruptly from the sea and its amazing interior with five lakes, numberless ponds and streams, varieties of flowers and birds.

Beyond and between these resorts are the nineteenth-century steamer stops—villages like Stonington, Christmas Cove and Cutler. Now too far off Route 1 for most motorists, they contentedly cater to yachtsmen, bicyclists and assorted escapists.

In one way or another these days tourism is the Maine Coast's chief industry, one closely linked to construction and real estate. More and more people, from everywhere it seems, are willing to pay a premium for an acre of coast. More than fifteen percent of the men and women you meet along the coast these days have moved here within the past decade. In Portland that adds up to a lot of people and a new look, a new life for the old port city.

Portland has, of course, been the most sophisticated and important city in northern New England since the 1820s—a status established during the grand age of sail and strengthened during the new state's lumbering and railroading eras, the last period being recalled in the elaborate brick buildings of the Old Port, a commercial area revitalized in the past decade, now a showcase for Maine's painters and craftsmen as well as its entrepreneurs.

Portland is still a city in which seagulls perch atop downtown skyscrapers (not too high, the human scale has not been lost) and there is a pervasive sense of sea. It's a city that prides itself on one of the country's most exquisite new museum buildings and one of New England's biggest civic centers, yet has dozens of islands within its limits—by-passed outcroppings of fir, rock and nineteenth-century cottages, still connected by regular ferry service to Custom House Wharf.

City man, island man, rich man (Maine has the third greatest concentration of millionaires in the country, most of them along the coast) and poor man (the state has the highest percentage of poor people in New England, many of them in coastal Washington County) all live—if you ask them—less 'on the coast' than 'on the ocean'.

Whatever the time of year the interplay between land and sea here holds rare beauty—the ocean itself may be just a dull grey but its crash against the rocks is a thing of splendor. By the same token a field of hay and pines which you wouldn't notice inland takes on extraordinary beauty when surrounded on three sides by water. A stand of fir is never more beautiful than on an island, with daisies and wild iris growing just below, and the pleasure of walking a pine-sided path is deepened by the tones of an off-shore buoy.

January 1984   CHRISTINA TREE

1 The bearded face of a Camden fisherman.

2 The Portland Observatory on Munjoy Hill is the last surviving nineteenth-century signal tower on the Atlantic. It commands a fine view of Portland and gives a sense of what it must have felt like to scan the horizon for a homecoming ship in the 1800s.

3 *(right)* A jogger sets out for an early morning run in the mist and spray, after a stormy night at Wells.

4 The late afternoon sun reflects in a cottage window on Monhegan Island.

5 A web of lines secures small boats to the wharf in Rockport at low tide.

6 Although the coastal region of Maine does not lend itself to a great deal of farming, every now and then one comes upon a massive New England barn such as this one in Brooksville.

7 *(right)* Autumn maples around a barn in Sedgwick.

8 *(left)* Few dining experiences are as rewarding as an evening picnic on a wharf, with fresh Maine lobster being served and the sun going down behind Boothbay Harbor.

9 Maine is well known for its craftsmen. Here coppersmith William McElvain proudly displays his hand-crafted copper and brass weathervanes in Searsport.

10 Newly painted lobster buoys await the winter season at Monhegan Island.

11 *(right)* West Quoddy Head light was built in 1809 at the most easterly point of the United States.

12 *(left)* Restaurant with a beautiful setting in Blue Hill.

13 A vintage car pulls out onto the street in Blue Hill.

14 View from Mt Cadillac, at 1532 feet the highest point on the eastern seaboard.

15 *(right)* Ellsworth Public Library is housed in the John Back Mansion, built as a wedding present in 1862; tradition has it that the bricks were brought by sea from Philadelphia.

16 *(left)* Two Lights State Park after a day of storm.

17 Fort Gorges, at Hog Island Ledge, Casco Bay, was built in 1858. This is the only major landmark in Maine that is named after Sir Ferdinando Gorges, an Englishman to whom most of Maine belonged as a proprietary colony in the early seventeenth century.

18 Entrance to a home in Northeast Harbour, Mount Desert Island.

19 *(right)* This ornate house in Kennebunk was built in 1826 and is known as the Wedding Cake House. Supposedly the bridegroom (a sea captain) had to rush off to sea before a wedding cake could be baked, but came back and made up for it later by so decorating his house.

20 *(left)* The rocky coastline of Mount Desert Island.

21 Perkins Cove is a much-painted man-made anchorage, a pleasant spot to walk around, with a drawbridge and a multitude of cluttered galleries and shops.

22 *(left)* A Boothbay flower garden over-flows with blossoms on a summer after-noon.

23 A quiet street corner in Castine. Situated on the Bagaduce Peninsula, this strategic port has changed hands between the English, French, and Dutch several times in the past three centuries and in 1779 was the last port to surrender to the Americans. Castine is now home to the Maine Maritime Academy.

24 *(left)* City Hall, Portland.

25 Drying newly-sewn sails at the Bohndell
Sails and Rigging Company near Rockport.

HARBOR

Candy Shop

26 Carved wooden signs, embellished with gold leaf, are a popular symbol of pride and individual craftsmanship in Maine.

27 *(right)* Geraniums in window boxes on a small bridge in East Blue Hill.

28 *(left)* Icy Atlantic waves pound the rocky shores of Mount Desert Island, Acadia National Park.

29 Pemaquid Point lighthouse seen from the ancient glacier-scarred rocks below.

30 *(left)* On an unusually warm afternoon in late winter a rugby team tosses the ball on Long Beach. In the distance, the cliffs of Cape Neddick are still covered in snow.

31 Tom McDermott's gilded ram sits atop Portland's First National Bank building. It replaced an almost 200-year-old wooden weather-cock.

32 Fort Popham, a semicircular granite fort, was built in 1861 near the
site of the unsuccessful Popham settlement of 1607.

33 Sunrise shines through the morning fog that rolls in from Belfast Bay.

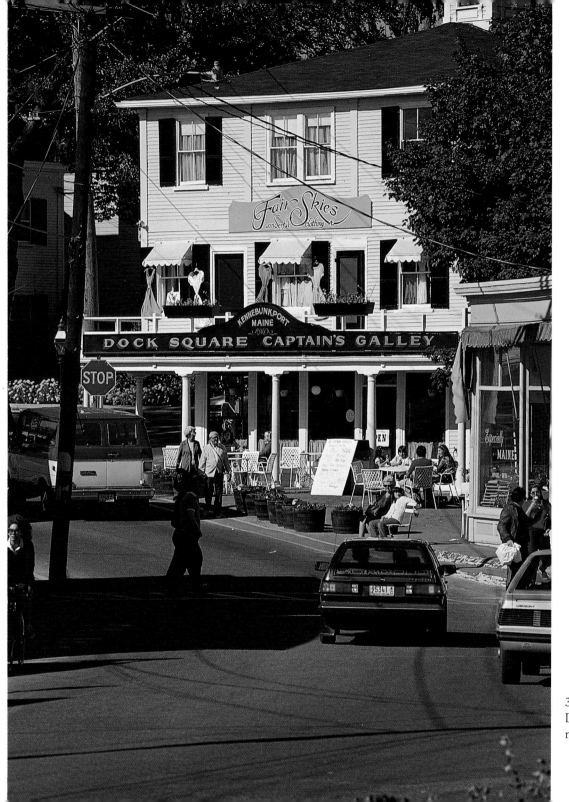

34 Kennebunkport is a popular resort town, Dock Square being one of the liveliest summer gathering spots in New England.

35 Fishing buoys and lobster traps decorate this weathered wharf-side building in Cape Porpoise.

36 Church steeple in Bath.

37 *(right)* Cape Elizabeth Light is one of the most powerful lights on the coast and replaced an earlier pair of lighthouses known as 'Two Lights', familiar to admirers of the painter Edward Hopper.

38 These three beautiful houses line a street of Calais on the Canadian border, where the St Croix River runs into the Bay of Fundy.

39 *(right)* A small pond near Wiscasset shortly after sunrise.

40 *(left)* The wealth and heritage of Camden were built around its shipbuilding industry and even today shipbuilding craftsmanship is handed on. View from the top of Mount Battie.

41 Rockport in winter.

42 Ice-fishing huts on the frozen surface of Jordan Pond, Acadia National Park.

43 Owl's Head Light, overlooking Penobscot Bay, sits on a cliff 100 feet above the sea. This handsome light was built in 1825.

44 *(left)* A small house surrounded by fall colors, Damariscotta.

45 The Thomaston Mansion, known as 'Montpelier'; originally built in 1794 by the Revolutionary War hero General Henry Knox and completely rebuilt as a works project in the Depression, financed by magazine publisher Cyrus Curtis.

46 *(left)* Black cat under a massive old tree in Friendship.

47 Lester Braddock near Thomaston; the early stages of carving an owl.
The Braddock brothers are well known for their decoys and bird carvings.

48 Cape Neddick light was built in 1879 on a small rock island that is separated from the mainland during high tides.

49 *(right)* Elegant homes, built overlooking the sea, reflect the grandeur and style of the 19th century York harbor where many wealthy summer residents built 'cottages' in the Yorks.

50 An abandoned house sits amid blueberry fields. In the distance the
Deer Island bridge spans Eggemoggin Reach to connect Little Deer Isle
with the rest of the East Penobscot region.

51 Winter sunrise over Searsport. Once a shipbuilding center, Searsport
is now a deepwater port and a pleasant town filled with mansions,
antique shops and inns.

52 The Carriage House Inn, Searsport, is one of the many fine old captains' houses and summer estates that have been converted into beautiful
inns along the coastline.

53 *(right)* Wooden fences line the peaceful streets of Castine.

54 As winter approaches, Camden's famous windjammer fleet is covered over for protection until spring, when the ships can resume their long sailing excursions.

55 Cadillac Mountain in Acadia National Park overlooks Mount Desert
Island. The first white man to visit the Island, Samuel de Champlain,
named it Ile des Monts Deserts (Isle of Bare Mountains).

56 Fishermen load modern lobster traps onto a fishing boat at Port Clyde.

57 *(right)* Climbers attempt to scale a massive ledge in Acadia National Park. The Park offers a wide variety of nature studies and outdoor activities.

58 Early risers stroll along a floating wharf in Southport, near Boothbay.

59 *(right)* With the right winter conditions Eagle Lake in Acadia National Park becomes an outdoor skating rink and a wide-open expanse for ice-boating.

60 The town clock near the park in
Bar Harbor.

61 *(right)* Islesboro lighthouse on Grindel
Point, Islesboro.

62 At the Portland ferry terminal, passengers wait for the boat to Peaks Island.

63 *(right)* Old Orchard Beach, a seaside amusement park.

64 The Cook's Lobster House on Bailey Island, seen from Orr's Island across the cut that is crossed by a unique cob-work or cribstone bridge, a structure of granite blocks laid so that they are held in place by their own weight.

65 Springtime along the waterfront in Bar Harbor.

66 Ocean rollers pound the breakwater that protects the summer homes near Wells.

67 *(right)* Portland Head Light was built on the orders of George Washington in 1791. It is the oldest light in Maine and a great place to picnic.

68 Early winter morning on York Harbor Beach.

69 *(right)* With the coming of fall, this Freeport lawn becomes a sea of red and orange.

70 *(left)* At low tide, the wharfs of Beals Island tower above the water. Beals Island is an unspoilt little island near Jamesport.

71 St Martha's Church reflected in the Kennebunk River, Kennebunkport.

72 *(left)* Wiscasset is a picturesque little town on the banks of the Sheepscot River. On a February afternoon dusk falls on the 18th-century buildings, sea-captains' houses, and the little churches, and recreates a scene from a bygone area.

73 Buckport bridge rises far above the Penobscot River and joins Verona Island with Stockton Springs. The mouth of the Penobscot was traditionally the end of the log run and before that the point at which ships bound for Bangor passed from the river into Penobscot Bay. Verona Island is an old ship-building site.

74 *(left)* Stonington, a fishing harbor on the tip of Little Deer Isle. At low tide, the harbor becomes a mass of rocky islands and stepping stones. Stonington is famous for its smooth, pink, granite rocks. The whole town, full of bright flowers, resembles a giant rock garden.

75 First Parish Congregational Church, Saco.

76 The giant crane of Bath Iron Works towers far above revitalized Front Street, Bath. The Bath Iron Works have been building United States Navy ships since the late 1800s.

77 *(right)* The Portland School of Art, Portland.

78 *(left)* Many of the shops in Dock Square, Kennebunkport, overlook the river. One can rent a canoe and spend the day paddling around and taking in the rustic charm.

79 Port Clyde, a small town at the tip of St George. From this wharf, the passenger ferry and mailboat is the lifeline joining Monhegan Island to St George and the mainland.

80 A cluttered assortment of shingled houses overlooking the harbor
gives Monhegan town its old and rustic charm. Monhegan House (on the
left) is the island's only large inn.

81 Nineteenth-century resort, Nonantum, looms over modern condo-
miniums above Ocean Avenue, Kennebunkport.

82 Early morning beachgoers relax in the sun at Kennebunk Beach.

83 *(right)* Sand Beach overlooking Newport Cove, Mount Desert Island;
one of very few beaches to be found in Acadia National Park.

84 East and west sides of Boothbay Harbor are connected by a long
wooden footbridge. A stroll along the bridge makes a quiet change from
the music and nightlife of a summer's evening in Boothbay.

85 This sailing enthusiast has escaped the crowded clubs and marinas. A stroll from the house to the cove brings him to his sailboat and he is free to sail from the mouth of Boothbay Harbor into the Gulf of Maine.

86 A Bucksport man makes a brave attempt to find his lawn under a foot of autumn leaves.

87 *(right)* A fiery sun disappears behind Kittery on an autumn evening.

88 Low tide, Old Orchard Beach.